MY DOG WASN't FAMOUS

But Let Me Tell You a Story About Her Anyway

Written and Illustrated by Billy O'Keefe

Cover design by Billy O'Keefe
Illustrations by Billy O'Keefe

ISBN: 9780988527300

First edition August 2017.

To Smiley the blind therapy dog, Fifty the two-legged pitbull, Leo & friends at the Old Friends Senior Dog Sanctuary, and the countless other older dogs, famous or not, who have dedicated their lives to brightening countless days for countless people.

A few years ago, while petting her head for probably the two millionth time, I felt a strange growth on the right side of Nina's forehead. It was small, roughly two-thirds the size of a pencil's eraser tip, but it was new and sudden. And, with Nina having accrued enough dog years to make such things increasingly worthy of concern, it was something worth monitoring.

A couple days later, the growth was marginally but undeniably larger, and accordingly more worthy of concern.
A precautionary vet appointment was made.

Then, suddenly, the following morning, she was gone.

Or he. Who knows.

I'm not qualified to discern whether the growth was male or female, but I **can** tell you it was not a growth, but a now-fully-grown tick who decided to leave its makeshift nest and go for a casual, meandering stroll a few inches from the right front paw of the dog upon whose head it had lived for half a week.

And there was Nina, attentively but lackadaisically watching it amble about — not wishing to bother it or eat it, not remotely enthralled by it, but just observing. I scooped the tick up, took it outside, and Nina put her head on her paw and dozed off, fully and characteristically oblivious to her role in raising that baby tick to become the conquering adult I set free into the world.

Though my work requires me to use it, I don't much like Facebook. Too much negativity, too much posturing, too much arguing about politics (don't get me started on that one), too many people talking at no one in particular instead of talking (and listening) to each other.

As a means to make myself dislike it less while enduring it, I began following a gradually alarming number of pages devoted to flooding my timeline with pictures and videos of famous, silly, insane and inspiring dogs who couldn't care less about politics and have no need to look smarter than everyone else. Perhaps you've muted half your friends list and done the same thing.

(I won't tell, don't worry.)

What I'm certain you have **not** done is seen this dog in any of those videos. Nina never traveled the world or hobnobbed with celebrities like Doug the Pug and Boo. She had no marketable skills — she never got a job even after turning 16 — and she never developed the kind of trick or vaguely-sounds-like-she's-saying-I-love-you bark that would provide the basis for a viral video. @WeRateDogs never rated her. She never even set up an Instagram account.

Such attention would have mortified her, if the lifelong cold war she dismissively waged against cameras was any indication. Didn't matter if it was a film camera, digital camera, camcorder or (eventually) smartphone — no matter the era or technology, Nina mastered the art of staring intently at the lens just long enough to fool me into pressing the button, only to turn her gaze anywhere but forward the split second the shutter clicked or the light illuminated. If you've seen a photo of Nina staring intently at a camera, what you aren't seeing is my hand holding a treat immediately behind it in an attempt to buy her cooperation.

(What you also don't see are the initial 15-20 attempted photos I'd previously taken of a dog's body with a blur for a head — assuming said head isn't halfway out of frame as she says "Forget this" and either reaches in for the treat or just walks away. Halfway around the globe, there are National Geographic photographers having easier times getting their subjects to play along.)

Technology in general mostly just confounded her. From remote control toys to stop-motion photography to touchscreen iPad pianos to my first FaceTime call, if it was new and novel to me, she often was my reluctant, eye-rolling test subject.

Some dogs run for the hills when noisy things they don't understand enter their space. Others turn to face them and make a pathetic attempt to bark them out of existence. Nina would just give whatever it was the side-eye, flash me a "Really, again?" glance, rise to her feet with the silent sigh of a mom constantly interrupting the dinner she made but cannot eat because an impatient child's juice cup needs refilling, and exit the room at a leisurely but unquestionably vexed pace — as if to say, "I'm going to go look out the window for a while. Please have this removed by the time I return."

End

Then, inevitably, barely two minutes later, her curiosity would consume her ("What if I can eat it?"), and she'd return to inspect the weird gizmo that casually chased her out of the room, conclude she could **not** eat it, but nevertheless indulge whatever silly idea I had before plopping back down on the floor and observing from a safe distance.

Do polite exasperation and camera-trolling count as tricks? I don't know, but it's as close as we're getting. Nina knew how to sit and lay down, but mostly did so when it aligned with her interests and not necessarily when commanded to. She came when you called her, but if you didn't have a treat or leash in hand, there was a better-than-insignificant chance she'd just go back to wherever she came from after weighing the pros and cons of sticking around. I never tired of watching the gears turn as, when deciding to leave instead of stay, she'd awkwardly walk backward for a few steps with a sorry-but-not-really look on her face before turning around and strolling away.

(Does a civil demonstration of independence count as a trick?)

She never learned to catch a frisbee or tennis ball, and it absolutely was for lack of trying. Toss a toy her way, and she usually just let it bounce off her head, sniff it to see if it was food, and resume licking whatever paw she was cleaning before the toy broke her concentration. One or two times — in her life, not in a play session — she would actually catch the toy in her mouth, but subsequent attempts proved this was merely an accident and not any sort of demonstration of intent.

Even fetch didn't quite work as I drew it up. Throw a ball past her, and if she was moved to chase it, she'd run after it, sniff it, look back at me as if to tell me, "Found your ball over here. Why do you keep losing it?" and then go eat some grass until I fetched and threw it again.

She was no dummy — she just decided this was how fetch best suited her. Chase ball, look at ball, look at me, eat a bunch of delicious grass, repeat. And because she was as stubborn as she was sweet, no one was going to change her mind.

When your dog is more
even-keeled than a saint and
twice as steadfast in her ways,
it's these little ticks — the
not-quite eye rolls, the awkward
saunters, the turning gears, the
occasional literal tick — that come to stand out over
time. Every dog has them, every dog's are unique,
and these, to me, are the stories from which a dog's
personality really shines through.

Take, for instance, this unremarkable story about basement stairs. For 12 years, we had a dog, Crystal, who descended them daily en route to the basement laundry room, which she'd decided as a young dog was going to be her bedroom (her bed being whatever pile of dirty clothes awaited her on the floor).

Nina inherited these stairs, and never once in her 16 years did she set paw on them. Something about their appearance — perhaps the way they twisted at the top, perhaps the gap in between each step — turned her off as a puppy, and her mind was made up for life.

But that didn't mean she wasn't curious about what was down there.

Almost without fail, regardless of where she was in the house, whenever I opened that basement door and walked downstairs, I could turn around a moment later and her head would be there — poking through the doorway as if it was a portal, performing some weird sniff of the air in hopes of gleaning valuable intel about the mysterious cavern into which I'd descended.

Upon returning to the surface, she'd still be there, ready to greet me with a chatty whimper that was — though one of many "talking" noises she made, especially in the latter half of her life — unique to that moment in terms of tone and tempo. I have no idea what she was trying to say, but she said it nearly every time.

And yes, Nina "talked" — not in a vaguely-sounds-like-words-people-say way, I'll reiterate, but absolutely in a fashion reminiscent of talking.

The noises she made were varied but unique to the events on which she was commenting — that accelerated string of half-yelps when I escaped the basement, an anticipatory not-quite singsong when first greeting her in the morning, a meandering conversational pattern for when she stood in a hallway between rooms and contemplated what to do next. There were numerous more, with each "sentence" sounding fundamentally similar but expressing something contextually distinct in much the same way our language and sentences do.

(My personal favorite: An escalating rush of joyous yelps, occasionally graduating to a pitchy bark and punctuated for whatever reason by a handful of quick sneezes, whenever I so much as pointed to her leash and signaled it was time for a walk.)

Her barks varied similarly, with different patterns and volumes for the mail carrier, the pizza delivery guy, people she encountered on walks, rival neighborhood dogs, and my car whenever it pulled up to the curb in front of the front door. (It's an ordinary black sedan with no obvious features to make it stand out from other black cars, but maybe my style of pulling up to curbs is unique, because she always somehow knew when it was my car and would always get up, approach the front screen door, and bark uncertainly under her breath until I got out of the vehicle and confirmed her hunch.)

Spend a decade and a half watching a dog develop mannerisms, routines and her own spoken language, and you even take notice of the things they don't say.

Such as how, whenever I gave her a post-walk treat, she would hold it in her mouth and take a few steps to walk away, but then turn around and stare at me until I removed my shoes.

Only after I complied, and she understood I wasn't going anywhere and that more playtime awaited, would she carry her treat into the den and eat it on the corner of carpeting she (and she alone) had decided was the spot where she'd eat treats.

(She cared less about eating her treat in the front hallway and leaving crumbs everywhere as she got older, but even then, shoes off first.)

Or, after I'd arrived at the house, the way she'd follow me into the kitchen and just stand there looking quizzically at me until I put some ice cubes in her water bowl and pointed to the bowl, which prompted her to walk over and look at it with a disingenuous curiosity, as if she didn't engineer the whole process, before taking a gulp.

Or when she'd go into the den and wait for everyone to join her at the time her body clock said was TV-watching time. Or the way she'd just casually hang around the kitchen when she was hungry for dinner, without ever making a fuss about being hungry. She never barked to get something, but instead just kind of shadowed people around the room with a masterful "Well? Is it ready yet?" face until she got her wish.

Such understated ways, which only increased in nuance as she aged, made Nina an ill fit for Internet fame. But her live audience was most appreciative. And the more she aged, the larger that audience grew.

If you've never watched a dog grow old, one of the things that might surprise you is just how significantly a little grey fur can reshape a dog's face and belie, rather than betray, their age. The deeper Nina ventured into her teenage years, the more paradoxically puppy-like her face became.

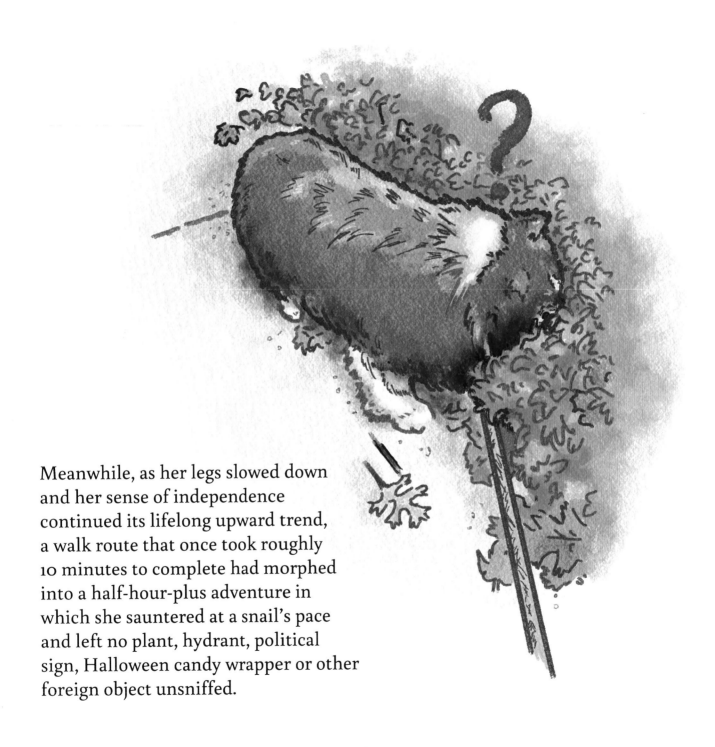

Meanwhile, as her legs slowed down and her sense of independence continued its lifelong upward trend, a walk route that once took roughly 10 minutes to complete had morphed into a half-hour-plus adventure in which she sauntered at a snail's pace and left no plant, hydrant, political sign, Halloween candy wrapper or other foreign object unsniffed.

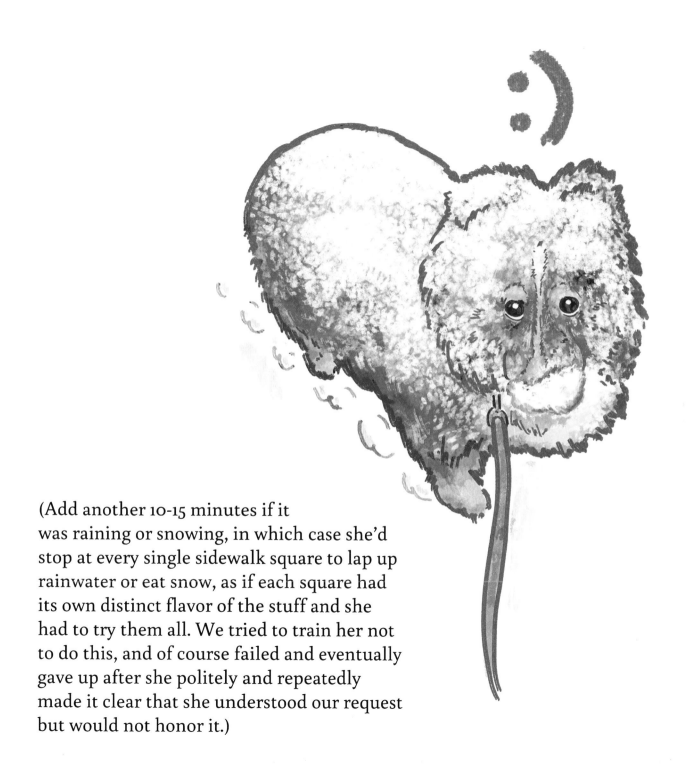

(Add another 10-15 minutes if it
was raining or snowing, in which case she'd
stop at every single sidewalk square to lap up
rainwater or eat snow, as if each square had
its own distinct flavor of the stuff and she
had to try them all. We tried to train her not
to do this, and of course failed and eventually
gave up after she politely and repeatedly
made it clear that she understood our request
but would not honor it.)

The sight of this puppy-faced dog traipsing so slowly down the block absolutely fascinated people. Probably a dozen times over the last couple of years, Nina literally stopped traffic as a car, driving past, would slow down and ultimately have to pull over so the driver or passenger could ask me whether she was one year old or 20.

When it wasn't cars, it was people — oftentimes folks on a walk who were a couple blocks behind us but inevitably caught and passed us, because walking as slow as Nina walked is humanly impossible unless you're indulging a dog who needs to know what's new with the shrub she's stopped to sniff at least 500 other times — who wanted to know her story.

(Nina, for her part, did what she did best — barked her who-is-this-stranger-on-my-private-sidewalk bark at them when they were 20 feet away, awkwardly but politely indulged them when they were close enough to pet her, and courageously resumed barking when they were too far away to pet her anymore. This phony act of bravery applied as well to dogs who scampered over to say hello, albeit with the addition of an "All right, get me out of this" glance she'd shoot my way whenever a dog sniffed her butt.)

If I was as good at speaking words off the cuff as I am at writing them after several rounds of editing, this is the story I would've told those folks. It most certainly is not an otherworldly story. But it is a story of a life well lived — 16-plus years of curiosity, discovery, silliness, stubbornness, quirkiness, deliciousness, happiness, love and affection as only a dog can show.

Remember that "Is dinner ready?" face I alluded to earlier? Nina had a similar but slightly different "Are you OK?" face that revealed itself at the uncanniest of times. Her gift for sensing unhappiness, frustration, doubt or discontent is nothing unique — dogs are masters at this, and if you show me someone who disagrees, I'll show you someone who has never been a dog's best friend.

What worked every time was the way she conveyed this sense that she knew something wasn't right — the same wide-eyed stare, accompanied by a dogged need to follow her troubled human but always somehow remain two feet in front of them, even if it entailed leaving one room and entering another and clumsily backing into who knows how many corners and walls along the way. She was not to be ignored.

(And yes, she had a special brand of talking for this occasion too.)

Only when you bent down to pet her head — to signal that you were all right, that everything would be all right, and that she's free to wag her tail and bury her head in your lap — did she let up. But by then, everything **was** better and **would** be all right.

I tend not to be a person easily dismayed by things, but it happens to all of us, and I never got over this phenomenon and how quickly it turned a bad day into a good one.

Nor will I ever not be thankful for it.

Nina O'Keefe was born on May 21, 2001 (probably — one of her birth certificates says May 22, but we're pretty sure that's a typo and not a birther conspiracy), and she spent 16 years and 55 happy days eating, sleeping, dreaming about eating, chatting, going on local adventures, playing with her monkey and Kong toys, occasionally acknowledging other toys, and generally brightening the days and nights of all who kept company with her.

She did not authorize this biography.

But I doubt she'd care it was made.

ABOUT THE AUTHOR

By day, Billy O'Keefe writes mostly unamusing web code. By moonlight, he is a writer and illustrator of delightful words and pictures. He enjoys both halves of his day. You can find samples of everything at his website, billyok.com.

Billy lives in Printers Row, Chicago, and **My Dog Wasn't Famous** is his second book. His first book, **These Are My Friends on Politics**, released in 2016.

CPSIA information can be obtained
at www.ICGtesting.com
Printed in the USA
LVXC01n1128110917
548260LV00001B/1